PN 6231 .D35 P54 1995
Pigeon, Annie.
A visitor's guide to the
 afterlife

The
Visitor's Guide to
The Afterlife

The
Visitor's Guide to
The Afterlife

Where to Go, What to Do,
Where to Eat,
And Other Heavenly
Hints

ANNIE PIGEON

KENSINGTON BOOKS

KENSINGTON BOOKS are published by

Kensington Publishing Corp.
850 Third Avenue
New York, NY 10022

Library of Congress Card Catalog Number: 94-073286
ISBN 0-8217-4987-0

First Printing: April, 1995

Printed in the United States of America

Dedicated to My Little Angel

Contents

Introduction

Once upon a time, life after death was one of those things everyone assumed would just sort of happen, and that not much advance planning was required. *Au contraire.*

Of late, the Afterlife has gotten a great deal of publicity. But it turns out there's a lot more to it than humdrum eternal bliss. The Afterlife is teeming with places to go, people to see, and things to do. Why miss out? If you're going anyway—and it's likely you are—you may as well be prepared.

This invaluable travel handbook will tell you everything you need to know about what's what in Eternity. You'll find everything from hints on dining and dancing hot spots, day excursions, and shopping expeditions to practical information on customs, currency, and climate.

So sit back, relax, and take an armchair voyage with the one and only official *Visitor's Guide to the Afterlife.* Before it's too late.

I

Things To Know
Before You Go

A Visitor's Query: Is it necessary to prepare in any way for going to the Afterlife, or can I just—as the saying goes—wing it?

The Guide Responds: Certainly plenty of people have taken off for the Afterlife on an impulse. Somehow they seem to get by. But it's always best to be prepared. It makes one's trip so much less stressful. Who wants to spend the first few eons in Eternity running around trying to find a well-stocked convenience store?

In the following pages you'll find tips on what to bring, what to leave behind, when the best time to go is, and what to expect in terms of weather.

What to Bring: The Basics

$3.50 in exact change for the Tunnel
▼
Number 45 or higher Paba-free sunscreen
▼
Ray-Bans
▼
Sheet music for "When the Saints Come Marching In"
▼
Lightweight, casual clothing
▼
Mousse (for limp halos)
▼
WD-40 (for stiff wings)
▼
American Express

Clearing Customs

Two pieces of checked luggage and two pieces of carry-on baggage may be taken by each visitor to the Afterlife. However, certain items are contraband:

You Can't Take It With You:

Fresh fruits or vegetables
▼
House plants
▼
Alcoholic beverages and other mind-altering substances
▼
Aerosol spray cans
▼
Books of existential philosophy
▼
Cigars
▼
Boom boxes
▼
Firearms with no legitimate sporting or recreational use
▼
Gifts Valued over $100

Please Note: Carry-on luggage must not exceed 9″ × 14″ × 22″. It is also inadvisable to take computer diskettes or unprocessed film through the Tunnel because, as the Toll Collector likes to joke, "God only knows . . ."

Necessary Documents

For admission to the Afterlife, it is necessary to prove that one, in fact, had a life. Hence, upon approach to the Tunnel it is incumbent upon the Traveler to present the following for inspection:

Birth Certificate
▼
Photo ID
▼
All Accumulated Diplomas
▼
Sample Pay Stubs, W2s, or 1099s
▼
Sample birthday cards, love letters, divorce decrees
▼
Assorted memos (E-mail okay)
▼
Proof of Address
▼
Recent Filofax
▼
Death Certificate (or Near-Death Certificate, as the case

may be)

Please note: Card-carrying atheists will be denied admission to the Afterlife.

The Climate

Heaven—Heaven is, as one would anticipate, mostly sunny. You may experience brisk breezes which serve to blow clouds about and to help propel pudgy cherubs. December brings snow—mostly for effect—but the rest of the time temperatures range from the mid to high 70s.

Limbo—Mostly overcast and drizzly. Seattle-like, only without a good coffee bar.

Hell—What did you expect? Hotter than blazes? Well, yes, but at least it's not humid. When the central air-conditioning is on it's quite comfortable indeed—and there's none of the harsh glare or stiff winds of Heaven to contend with. Of course, the central air isn't *always* on . . .

When To Go

When your kids start looking at nursing homes.

▼

When you overhear your doctor say, "If he recovers he'll

be a vegetable."

▼

When Willard Scott wishes you Happy Birthday for the

second time.

▼

When your margin calls come in after a market crash.

▼

When you'd rather die than compromise.

▼

When you'd rather die than quit smoking.

▼

When you're ready for your close-up, Mr. DeMille.

Directions to the Afterlife

Fasten seat belt.
▼
Go straight up and continue until you enter a vortex.
▼
Go through toll booth. (Have exact change ready.)
▼
Enter Tunnel. Put on Ray Bans.
▼
Exit at light. Take a left at the harps.
▼
When you see the pearly gates, honk.

II

Settling In

A Visitor's Query: Entering Eternity is certainly a little overwhelming. Can you help me get a handle on what's going on?

The Guide Responds: The Afterlife is just like any busy destination in that visitors feel a little disoriented at first. This section will tell you how to get around and how to find suitable lodging. It will also answer your questions about Eternity's economy, and employment opportunities in the angelic hierarchy.

Getting Around

Saint Christopher's Cabs—Since being decanonized, the deposed but determined angelic bigwig whose image hung on so many dashboards for so many years is staging a grassroots comeback in the transportation field. His livery service offers courteous, dependable transport at a reasonable price. (When asked whether he thinks he can regain his former stature, Chris is sure to reply, "Look what happened to Donald Trump.")

Swing Lo Sweet Chariots—This upscale fleet offers stretch chariots equipped with minibars, VCRS, and state-of-the-art cellular phones. Pricey, a little snooty, but all in all quite the trip.

Cloud Nine Express—For those who want to economize, this shuttle bus will carry riders to their destination for a mere pittance—albeit with minimal amenities. (Hence the company's slogan "No snacks, no wine. No frills. Cloud Nine.") A wonderful choice of travel for the meek and the humble.

Soul Train—By far the most widely used of the heavenly transportation options, this regally restored period locomotive squires myriad former earthlings to their destinations daily. You're sure to run into old friends and make new ones as the Soul Train glides along its heavenly way.

Bethlehem Rent-A-Star—Still trying harder, even unto death, this feisty firm provides reasonably priced steer-them-yourself, four-on-the-floor meteors. Be sure to pick up a map at the rental counter.

Accommodations

The Ark—This former cruise ship turned permanently docked "floating hotel" is unique. If you and a significant other are looking for a place to get comfy and cozy this "couples-only" retreat may be just the spot. But keep your stay relatively short. The lions are bossy. The hyenas are noisy. And after a while, even the pandas become tedious. (Moderate/Expensive)

Tower of Babble—A favorite stomping ground for Eternity's international jet set, this high-rise luxury hotel boasts a sophisticated, multicultural clientele. Knowledgeable and helpful staff cater to special needs in all languages, however billing can be confusing. And unless you take a crash course in Speaking in Tongues, you will lack for lively conversation around the pool. (Expensive)

The Holy Day Inns—A clean and respectable chain with uninspired decor and somewhat sluggish service. Choose a Holy Day Inn when you need a place to hang your halo and don't expect to be spending much time in your room anyhow. (Moderate)

The "No Room at the Inn" Inn—It is a delight to lodge at this charming but exclusive bed and breakfast. Just follow that very bright star to its front door—*if* you've called ahead for a reservation. If not, you'd better take that No Vacancy sign seriously. With its heavenly quaintness, first-rate morning cappuccino and fresh-baked croissants, it's usually booked lifetimes in advance. (Expensive. No family rates available.)

Club Dead—This all-inclusive Mediterranean-style resort offers something for everyone, whether you're a would-be "cloud potato" or the sort who likes to pack a day chock full of everything from windsurfing to conga dancing. Of course, you'll be chided if you fail to participate in silly group activities and sing the official Club Dead anthem, "Rock of Ages." Nevertheless, a real value. (Moderate. Club Dead "money beads" accepted.)

Nearer My God To Thee—This modest motel is often filled to capacity, and not because of its decor or amenities. Its surefire secret: Location, location, location. As a newcomer to the Afterlife, you simply can't park yourself any closer than this to the Big Kahuna, the Guy in Charge, the Absolute Almighty Himself. The upside of this, of course, is that when your Day of Judgment comes and you have to stand before Him, you won't have far to go. The downside: Nearer My God To Thee has no HBO in its rooms (something about interference from nearby angelic auras). (Moderate/Expensive)

The Local Economy

Answers to the most frequently asked questions about financial life in the Afterlife:

Q. *Will I actually need money in Eternity?*
A. Get real. How do you think the Almighty takes care of all His overhead?

Q. *Do I have to bring cash, or is credit okay?*
A. The Almighty is not picky, however credit makes for easier bookkeeping. And even the Good Lord *hates* pennies, not to mention those stupid Susan B. Anthony dollars.

Q. *What should I do if I left home without my American Express?*
A. Visa has certainly made lots of inroads in Heaven in recent years but at some of its more upscale dining establishments and five-star hotels old standards die hard.

Q. *Will my code from earth still work in Heaven's ATMs?*
A. No. In order to extract money from Heaven's automated tellers you'll need to punch in the correct answer to "How many angels can dance on the head of a PIN?"

Q. *Are there income and sales taxes in the Afterlife?*
A. Well, technically we would have to say no. However,

the Almighty *strongly* suggests an income "tithe" of 33 percent and a sales "tithe" of 7 percent.

Q. *How strongly does He suggest it?*
A. Let's put it this way. Job didn't take Him seriously and . . .

Q. *If I'm going to be in Eternity forever, won't I need an awful lot of money?*
A. You betcha. Of course you will earn some income from performing your angelic duties, as described on the following page. But investing wisely is really the key. One thing you can say for Heaven, it's possible to buy low and sell high. Very, very high. (However, we suggest you steer clear of Eternal Life Insurance policies. You pay premiums indefinitely and never get to collect.)

Who's Who in Heaven:
Some Job Descriptions

A rose is a rose is a rose . . . but an angel can be many things. In Heaven, as it was on Earth, it's best to know just who you're dealing with. And if you're wondering what openings are available once you've got your wings, here's the lowdown:

Seraphim—The highest order of the Almighty's servants. The primary job description of the Seraphim is to chant a song of creation over and over again. Applicants for the job must have: An ability to carry a tune, a taste for redundancy.

Cherubim—A notch under Seraphim in the Heavenly hierarchy, the job of the chubby Cherubs is to bear the Lord's throne and drive His Chariot. They moonlight by ornamenting cathedral ceilings. Applicants for the job must have: Driver's license, chauffeur's cap, love handles.

Dominations—This order of angels is in charge of regulating other angels' duties. Think of them as middle management. Applicants for the job must have: a laptop with Excell spreadsheet, copy of *The Saint Peter Principle*. MBAs preferred.

Virtues—These "angels of grace" bestow blessings from above and specialize in instilling courage in whoever should need it. Applicants must have: An inclination to stick their nose into other people's business and good timing.

Powers—These angels are the heavenly border patrol, keeping pesky demons at bay. In heavenly lore they are variously known as the Dynamis, the Authorities, and, of course, the Power Rangers. Applicants must have: Excellent night vision, combat fatigues. Patriot Missile training a plus.

Archangels—Messengers who carry Divine decrees, these high-profile angels are the chief intermediaries between man and his Maker. Applicants must have: Access to the Internet, star quality and call waiting.

Charlie's Angels—Glamorous pursuers of bad guys and solvers of whodunits. Applicants must have: Big hair.

III

Fine Dining

A Visitor's Query: I find I've worked up quite an appetite while getting acclimated. Where can a person get a decent meal around here?

The Guide Responds: The Afterlife is rife with restaurants, many of them excellent choices for the hungry Heavenly novice. Feast your eyes on the following listings . . .

Dining Out

The Last Supper—This casual eatery just inside the gates is where those who did not have time to order a final meal before departing Earth get to sample that "down-home" cooking one more time. Whether your favorite earthly repast was Mom's tapioca pudding, Uncle Bob's three-alarm chili, or Grandma's long-simmering Sunday spaghetti sauce, the staff serves it up with panache. (Moderate)

Cumulus—Formerly the Cloud Café and now under new management, this chic bistro merits that much overused heavenly adjective: divine. No mere words can describe its Ambrosia Antipasto and its Cold Nectar Bisque. So, just sing hallelujah! (Very Expensive)

The Serenity Spa Restaurant—Renowned for its satisfying yet slenderizing "Light" cuisine, this is spa dining at its best. Try the pasta primavera—angel-hair of course. (Expensive)

Burned at the Steak—Saint Joan of Arc's whimsical theme restaurant offers charbroiled favorites amidst a decor that pays homage to misunderstood martyrs of all persuasions, proving once and for all that in Heaven everyone has a sense of humor—and a merry disregard for clogged arteries. (Moderate/Expensive)

Manna Mania—Need a quick fix in the middle of a long trek. Enjoy miraculously fast food that hits the spot. The chicken is addictive—especially the wings. (Inexpensive)

Bacchus—The incomparable libations at this wine bar simply defy belief. Named for its chief sommelier, a veritable Greek God (sure to turn the heads of lady patrons), it has offered the best in wine and spirits for the past several eons. (Expensive)

Nirvana—The great Hindu gods, in all their incarnations, are said to frequent this fine Indian dining establishment. But the curry is so spicy ("Hotter than Hades," the gods have been said to jest) that chances are you'll be too busy fanning yourself to notice. (Moderate)

Valhalla—This final outpost of the chain begun by the "Viking Gourmet" features Norse morsels amidst a decor of murals of great warriors fallen in battle. A popular hangout for the Grunge crowd; best skipped by everyone else. (Inexpensive/Moderate)

Holy Molé—Out-of-this-world Mexican fare in a festive setting. Wash it down with a Corona Light. (Moderate/Expensive)

Loaves and Fishes—Lox and bagels—what else?—are standard fare at this casual and colorful 24-hour deli. (Moderate)

Planet Afterlife—Ancestors of Sly Stallone and Bruce Willis run this touristy, overpriced hamburger joint for the would-be stargazers of Heaven. But do you really need a sweatshirt with their logo? We don't think so. (Too Expensive)

Angel Food—This dessert shop and ice cream emporium features treats which in any other milieu could only be described as "sinfully delicious." Be sure to try the Pope Tarts and Apple St. Crispin. Make a special effort to drop in at the annual Angel Food Cake Bake-Off. Of course, you simply must indulge in the *specialité de la maison,* Death by Chocolate (the recipe for which is so commonly requested that we are reprinting it on the following page, along with another heavenly favorite, Serenity Spa's Angel-hair Pasta Primavera)

Death by Chocolate

(Because, hey, what have you got to lose?)

  32 lbs. unsalted butter, melted
    8 gallons heavy cream
    4 gallons crème de cacao
       pinch of vanilla
  15 lbs. granulated sugar
  10 large bars unsweetened chocolate, melted
  10 bags Nestlé chocolate chip morsels, softened
  10 lbs. confectioners' sugar

In large bathtub, combine butter, cream, crème de cacao, and vanilla.

With large shovel, add granulated sugar. Stir.

With trowel, blend in melted baker's chocolate and chocolate morsels.

Sprinkle with confectioners' sugar.

Ease self into tub, submerge and and enjoy. Serves 1.

CAUTION: Recipe works only at Heavenly altitude. *Do not try this at home.*

Serenity Spa's Angelhair Pasta Primavera

one dozen angels
barber shears
broccoli
plum tomatoes
olive oil
parmesan

Toss broccoli, tomatoes, and olive oil.
Sprinkle with parmesan.
Persuade angels they need a trim.

IV

Where the Action Is

A Visitor's Query: Dinner was delicious. But now I'm up for some fun. What's to do around here for recreation and entertainment? I hope you're not going to tell me to say my prayers and go straight to bed?

The Guide Responds: There's so much to keep one amused in the Afterlife it's hard to choose from among the many activities. The following pages will outline some highlights in everything from clubs, casinos, and cinema to live music and spectator sports.

And for those evenings when you decide you're just too pooped to party, we've added some TV listing highlights.

Nightlife After Death

The Big Bang—This "bowling alley at the end of the Universe" is the setting for a fun, affordable, and generally stellar evening.

Heaven's Gate Movie House—Ancestors of star-crossed director Michael Cimino run this popular big-screen theater featuring retrospectives of big budget films that "died at the box office." (If you missed *Ishtar* on earth, don't let it happen again!) Try the popcorn with extra butter. Remember, you're already history.

The Burning Bush—Rave all night at this on-the-edge dance club—if you can get in, that is. The doorman here is so selective he makes Saint Peter seem like a pushover. Only the hippest of the departed can get past him, though a pierced halo or tattooed wing will help your chances. Amazing enough, even the Creator himself was once turned away on a busy Saturday night. Plague and pestilence followed, of course, but all has since been forgiven.

Holy Rollers—Whether roulette or blackjack is your game, or if you simply prefer the slots, you'll find action a-plenty at this glamorous casino. Try out your lucky numbers. But remember: Sooner or later, the House always wins.

Music, Music, Music

You thought it was all the Hallelujah Chorus and Mass in B Minor. Well, sure, in Eternity one can go-for-Baroque all the time if that's your thing. But, as the Almighty has been heard to quip, "Hold my soul, well I sure am fond of my rock and roll. . . ."

If you're like-minded, be sure to check out the following acts that appear regularly at The Burning Bush and other trendy venues:

The King is Dead—We know, we know. Elvis is allegedly still back on Earth, and was recently cited at a 7–11. Well, if you believe that we've got a nice piece of swamp land in Limbo we'd like to sell you. The truth is, the King is swiveling his way through Eternity and, with his host of angelic impersonators, sells out Caesar's routinely. Granted, he's been a tad upset about the whole Michael Jackson/Lisa Marie thing lately, but the Colonel assures us he'll be back on his feet in no time . . .

The Seriously Grateful Dead—Ancestors of Jerry Garcia and company bring the house down with their Live Dead concerts, though—strangely enough—their albums have never managed to capture their infectious energy. If you're a seriously real Dead Head your best bet is to get on board the "Follow the Dead" Bus and boogie through Eternity with a backstage pass.

Apocalypse—Jim Morrison and Janis Joplin front this amazing supergroup with Jimi Hendrix and Brian Jones on guitars. Most requested numbers include "Break On Through to the Other Side" and "Oh, Lord Won't You Buy Me a Mercedes-Benz."

Teen Angels—Ancestors of the Shangri-La's sing Top 40 nostalgia favorites from The Heavenly Hit Parade.

Road Kill—Heaven's premier Grunge group for the nose ring crowd.

The Sporting Afterlife

World Chalice Soccer—Europe and Latin America's hottest sport has finally begun making some inroads in Heaven, and now *everyone* wants to win the prized chalice. But watch out for those fans. There's nothing pretty about being trampled by horde of overly zealous cherubim.

Field of Dreams Baseball—Babe Ruth, Jackie Robinson, Shoeless Joe Jackson, and friends face off in ultimate Dream Teams. Unfortunately, the players have been on strike for ages. Fans are praying for Almighty arbitration.

Archangels on Ice—Wee! You've never seen an ice show like this. Triple lutzes! Quadruple spins! Ten Lords a Leaping! Legions of Snow Angels glide along in the Angelic Ice Parade, with commentary by David Letterman's great-great-grandmother.

The Annual Supernova Bowl—Football fans rejoice. Your annual January ritual is still alive—so to speak—bigger and better than ever. Winning teams receive Supernova rings. Losers are swallowed up by a black hole.

Eternal Masters Gold Tournament—For all you golf lovers who thought earthly pro tournaments always ended too soon, this is your green come true. So, relax and enjoy—you've got all the time in the world, and then some . . .

What's on TV in Eternity?

It's A Wonderful Afterlife—Can a genuinely nice guy, with the help of a bumbling but well-meaning angel, triumph over a smarmy little banker out to destroy his corner of Heaven? What do *you* think? Jimmy Stewart will star in this upcoming series based on the popular earthly flick. Well worth defecting from the Devil's contender in this time slot, *Murder, She Wrote*.

Dead with Regis and Kathie Lee—Perky, but self-absorbed Hosts preside over this daily chat/variety potpourri featuring guest spots with famous dead and near-dead celebrities. Next week: Marilyn Monroe, the original Lassie, and Dick Cavett.

Extreme Northern Exposure—A cast of zany characters populates a one-horse town in Limbo while they wait for their contracts to expire.

Sixty Minutes in Heaven—Sanctimonious investigative reports shamelessly grill interview subjects until they beg for mercy. Fortunately, this being Heaven and all, mercy is available. Also: Deadly dull "humor" commentator poses such questions as: "Didja ever wonder why there's so much junk mail in the Afterlife?"

Eternitysomething—Yuppies in Paradise. Will they finally stop whining? Tune in next week. . . .

I Love Saint Lucy—On Earth, third-century A.D. martyr St. Lucilla may have been best known for good works. But in Eternity she's renowned for her wacky stunts and wild plots to foil her bandleader husband and break into show business by hook or by crook. A Heavenly hoot.

Wheel of Heaven—Divine Word puzzles for the brain dead. The key attractions are the outfits on the pretty, blonde angel who spells out the answers. Prizes, prizes, prizes!

Infinity 90210—Intrigues of the rich and the restless in the Afterlife's snazziest zip code.

Saturday Night Dead—While not as uproarious as it once was, this irreverent weekly comedy grab bag still has its moments, especially now that Belushi is back. Also, the Almighty gets quite a chuckle out of the Church lady.

Baywatch—Heavenly bodies.

V

Local Customs

A Visitor's Query: Sometimes I feel a bit like a fish out of water in the Afterlife. I'm always afraid I might do or say the wrong thing. Can you give me some hints on etiquette?

The Guide Responds: We know correct behavior is of concern to our visitors. You definitely do not want to offend anyone in Eternity. In the following pages you'll learn: what to expect at local festivals and celebrations; suggested conversational-starters when chatting with saints and prophets; the correct form for Heavenly thank you notes; and—most important of all—how to conduct yourself on your Day of Judgment.

Festivals and Special Events

Fourth of July Fireworks—Comets, super-novas, galactic implosions, meteor showers. The Almighty pulls out all His stops for this bedazzling annual jubilee. (Occasionally Jupiter gets sideswiped, but what the hey . . .) Bring your picnic blanket and cooler along and be sure to stick around for the finale, wherein the Milky Way is temporarily rearranged in the shape of Mickey and Minnie Mouse, rendering Galileo speechless.

Presidents Day—Washington, Lincoln, Jefferson join more recently departed leaders of the free world for a day of celebration. This is your chance to sing "Hail to the Chiefs," meet and greet your favorite Democrats and/or Republicans and get answers to all the questions you secretly wanted to ask in history class. ("Like, wow, how'd you keep your *balance* while crossing the Delaware?"; and "Did you really think anyone would buy that Rosemary Woods thing?") Alternate side of the galaxy parking suspended.

All Saints Day (Halloween)—See your favorite holy men and women "lighten up" and take a day off from their busy schedule of miracle working. Pious do-gooders? Not today! Today they're pirates and cowboys, gypsies and gnomes clamoring, "Trick or treat!" Devil costumes are frowned upon.

Labor Day—The Good News: In Heaven after this summer's end holiday, you can still wear white.

Christmas—Earthly Yuletide, for all its fun, had its share of minor annoyances. In Heaven, however, Christmas is perfection itself. Your tree doesn't tilt, your lights don't short circuit, and your eggnog doesn't curdle. All your gifts are just what you always wanted and batteries are always included.

New Year's Eve—"Should old acquaintance be forgot" . . . Well, just you never mind about that ditty. All your old acquaintances are here in the Afterlife, and on New Year's Eve they all gather in Beyond Times Square to elbow one another and sport party hats atop their halos. At the stroke of midnight there's a group hug followed by a cosmic yawn.

Thanksgiving—You can eat all you want at this yearly feast, but you may find it hard to obtain lift-off afterward, especially if you're not really used to your wings yet. Better to hold off on that second helping of stuffing and spend some time engaging in Thanksgiving's more politic Heavenly ritual. This is the day to write a thank-you note to your guardian angel, expressing gratitude for all he or she did for you while you were Earth-Bound. If you're somewhat uneasy about performing this task, fear not. An all-purpose format is presented on the following page. . . .

"Dear Guardian Angel . . ."

A Sample "Thank You" Note

Dear *(Insert Name of Angel)*:

How lucky I was to have you hovering over my shoulder for *(Insert Number of Years Spent on Earth)*. Without your support and guidance I'm sure I never would have *(Insert Appropriate Accomplishment, e.g. "won the Sixth Grade Science Fair trophy;" "met Ms./Mr. Right;" "trimmed down to a size 14.")*

There were many times I could have sworn I heard your wise voice whispering in my ear. (Thanks for that stock tip.) Then there was the day you really saved my hide. I'll never forget when you rescued me from the *(Insert Deathly Menace of Choice, e.g. "falling piano"; "poison dart"; "out-of-control tractor trailer")*. Quick thinking, G.A.!

Of course, I wouldn't be here now if you hadn't slipped up a little bit. But I guess everyone deserves a *(Insert Rationalization of Choice, e.g. "long lunch hour"; "personal day"; "nap")* once in a while. Hey, who's complaining? At least we meet at last.

Yours truly,
(Your Name Here)

Some Do's and Don'ts
of Celestial Small Talk

If you meet Moses, ask to see his Red Sea slides.

If you run into Saint Francis of Assisi, tell him about that cute little shepherd you adopted at the ASPCA.

If you come across Saint Jude, tell him how much you liked that Beatles song.

If you meet Saint Thomas Aquinas, tell him you think teachers are underpaid.

If you meet the Buddha don't offer him your copy of *Thirty Days to a Flatter Tummy*.

If you meet Krishna, don't hold him accountable for all those times you were harassed at airports.

Never, never offer Saint Peter a gratuity.

More Heavenly Etiquette

Top Excuses For Your Day of Judgment

Anxious about how to account for those little indiscretions, teeny-weeny white lies, and minor felonies you may have committed during your Life on Earth? Not to worry. Our survey has determined the following explanations tend to go over best with the Almighty . . .

1. I ate too many Twinkies.

2. My mother potty trained me too early.

3. Watched too much *NYPD Blue*.

4. Wanted to appear on tabloid TV.

5. Hoped to meet Alan Dershowitz.

6. Oh, were there *ten* Commandments?

Of course, these tend to work only if the Almighty is having a very good day. See the next page for hints on how to tell . . .

How To Read the Almighty's Mood

Top Signs the Almighty is Having a Nice Day

1. He looks at all He's created and decides it is Good

2. He's humming, "Om, what a beautiful morning."

3. He schedules a portrait sitting with Michelangelo.

4. He creates something amusing, like the duck-billed platypus or the House of Windsor.

5. He's holding orchestra seats to *Godspell*.

Top Signs the Almighty is Having a Bad Day

1. He wonders aloud if he was too soft on Job.

2. He tries to sell you flood insurance.

3. He complains that even on the Seventh Day he didn't get any rest.

4. He complains that One is the loneliest number.

5. He's been beaten at poker by Charles Darwin, Frederick Nietzsche, and Sigmund Freud.

VI

Side Trips

A Visitor's Query: Is there more to the Afterlife than just Heaven? And, if so, can I visit these other locales?

The Guide Responds: Absolutely. During your stay in the Afterlife you may wish to plan excursions to such exotic destinations as the Garden of Eden, Limbo and, of course, the legendary Hell. See what follows for some tips as to how to get the most out of these fun and educational side trips.

Things To See and Do
in the Garden of Eden

Hermès Snakeskin Boutique—Sturdy handbags, luggage, briefcases and, of course, très chic belts and pumps can be purchased here, though some say the prices made their skin crawl. (For heavenly discounts, refer to our Dying to Shop section.)

Eve's Apple Stand—You'll be sorely tempted by fruit-filled pies, turnovers, pancakes, blintzes, crepes, and fritters. For your beverage, sample cider so sweet it will bring a lump to your throat.

Adam's Ribs—This unique concession stand features scruptious baby-backs. Wednesday is ladies night.

Tree of Knowledge—The Garden's game show. Thrill to this eternally engaging tournament of champions. But please, those of you who participate, remember to phrase your responses in the form of a question. Penalty for not doing so is expulsion from the Garden.

My Original Sin—A parfumerie par exellence. Don't leave without treating yourself to some of the exquisite—but naughty—namesake fragrance.

Ten Ways To Pass Time in Limbo

1. Thumb through old *Newsweek*s and *Fortune*s

2. Solve Rubik's Cube

3. Try to remember all seven Deadly Sins

4. Try to remember all seven Heavenly Virtues

5. Try to remember all Seven Dwarves

6. Tune in to the Weather Channel

7. Pal around with the ex-communicated

8. See how long you can hold your breath

9. Help your Chia pet grow.

10. Watch the *Twighlight Zone* marathon.

To Hell and Back:
What Dante Didn't Tell You

Back on earth, "Go to Hell" was generally considered a rude and dismissive remark, roughly equivalent to the more colloquial "Blow it out your ear." In the Afterlife, however, advising a visitor to "go to Hell" is really more of a helpful travel tip, roughly equivalent to a Parisian advising a foreign visitor to go to the top of the Eiffel Tower. The good news: Hades is a scintillating destination full of amazing attractions and interesting people. And no one stays forever, at least not since rent control laws were overturned in the early 14th century (too late, alas, for the industrious but now badly outdated Dante to incorporate into his opus). The bad news: It seems like everyone is going to Hell these days, so expect long lines and crowds—even worse than at Disneyworld.

Hell's Hot Spots

River Styx Dayliner—Boatman Charon can be a moody sort, but that doesn't prevent this three-hour cruise from being one of Hell's highlights.

Seven Sins Theme Park—Despite the name, there's fun for the whole family at this well-run establishment. Try the Pride Slide, the Envy-Go-Round, the Wheels of Wrath, and the Avarice Avalanche (watch out for those flying nickels!). Parents will want to park the kids for a bit at McGlutton's Burger Emporium while they make a fast dash for the Lust Log Flume. When your busy day's all done, you can reunite for a snooze at Sloth Central.

Persephone's—You recall this famous mythological cutie, kidnapped by the lord of the Underworld and doomed to dwell there for part of each year. Sounds like a drag, doesn't it? Well, that's what *she* thought until she opened this renowned beauty and skin care salon. Try the manicure/pedicure combo, or, if you can spare the time, spring for the Day From Hell Special Treatment, which includes facial, eyebrow wax, and a *very* long rest on a tanning bed.

Hot to Trot—This delightful art deco-style ballroom is Hell's hoppin' spot for tripping the light fantastic. Do a steamy bossa nova with your date, or burn up the rug with a daring tango. If you're feeling really naughty, the lambada is still "in" in Hades.

Firewalker's—Sit back and sip a hot toddy while you wait your turn to traverse beds of flaming coals. Be sure to bring your super strength Aloe lotion.

The Devil Made Me Do It—Passes to tapings of this popular talk show are hotter than Letterman tickets, so write *way* in advance of your journey (or bribe an usher). Once in the doors, you'll have a bird's-eye view as guests bare their souls about what heinous deeds they committed at the behest of Satan. Lots of tears, lots of levity ensue. All followed by warm (very warm) hugs.

Bosch's Boutique—An art gallery well worth browsing through and a fab place to pick souvenir posters and post-cards of all Hell's prime attractions.

Hell in a Handbasket—*The* place for crafts.

Who's Who in Hell:
A Nine Rings Update

	Dante's 13th Century	*Late 20th Century*
Circle One:	Virtuous Unbaptised	Spent Sunday Mornings with Charles Kuralt
Circle Two:	Lustful	Accused of Sexual Harassment
Circle Three:	Gluttonous	Didn't Give Doggie Bag to the Doggie
Circle Four:	Avaricious	Wouldn't Give at the Office
Circle Five:	Wrathful	Never Been to Therapy
Circle Six:	Heretics	Politically Incorrect
Circle Seven:	Violent	Never Been on Prozac
Circle Eight:	Hypocrites, Thieves	Congress
Circle Nine:	Traitors	Voted for Perot

VII

Shopping

A Visitor's Query: It sounds like I can pick up some cute little knickknacks in Hades, and some expensive goodies in the Garden of Eden. But surely there must be some good discount shopping in Heaven.

The Guide Responds: Indeed! If you have spent your life dying to shop, Heaven is the place for you. On the following pages we highlight some of its most irresistible outlets.

Bargains to Die For

Shoes of the Fisherman—Footwear, luggage, and other leather goods. Knockoffs of snakeskin bags and belts that look so much like the expensive version in the famed Garden of Eden Hermès boutique that only a Supreme Being could tell the difference. Also, the best deal in town on Water-walkers hightops.

The Good Book—Thirty percent off hardcover versions and twenty percent off all paperback versions of New Testaments, Old Testaments, and Slightly Used Testaments.

Last Writes—Stationery, fountain pens, markers, elegantly bound blank journals, and the like. In short, all the literary paraphernalia you'll need to begin writing your own bestseller on your experience in the Afterlife—or simply to drop a postcard from the edge.

God Bless You—Discount Drugs, specializing in over-the-counter cold and allergy medication. You may find it comes in handy, since those clouds can get drafty, and since newcomers to the Afterlife often react intensely to the pollen count from the many varieties of flowers in the Garden.

Heaven Scent—High-quality imitation designer fragrances at prices that will make your spirits soar. You can't get the authentic My Original Sin here, but you can get a copy that's almost as deliriously sensuous.

Paradise Lost and Found—This consignment shop offers a potpourri of vintage treasures, such as recycled archangel staffs and robes, gently used Hell's Angel's leather jackets, and adorable little papal caps.

Shrouds of Turin—Designer duds at prices that are out of this world.

Bringing in the Sheaves—Food co-op specializing in grain products. Bulk barrels of wheat, oats, barley, and rye are great bargains, if you're the type who likes to make your own granola. (Although, health food didn't really keep you out of the Tunnel, now, did it?) At the very least, try the homemade muffins. Loaded with butter, but at this point *who cares?*

Siddhartha—Incense, candles, chant CDs, and assorted esoterica make for fun browsing in this Buddhist boutique.

Karma-Mart: The "Get-A-Life" Specialists—If you're thinking of reincarnating, this is simply *the* place to outfit yourself for your next life. Whether you'll be returning as a society belle, a Five Star General, or—that perennial favorite—a member of Ancient Egyptian royalty, Karma Mart's got everything you'll need.

Mine Eyes Have Seen the Glory—Optometrists. Wide selection of designer frames. Free exam.

This Little Light of Mine—Lamps.

VIII

Staying Healthy

A Visitor's Query: What's the secret to staying fit and trim after death? Must I still watch my cholesterol? How about diet and exercise—still necessary, or can I finally kick back and relax?

The Guide Responds: Happily, in the Afterlife cholesterol counts no longer count. After all, what are you going to have—a heart attack? *However*, the truth is residents of Heaven really can put on the pounds (if you don't believe this, take a gander at the Sistine Chapel). You'll really enjoy Eternity much more if you make an effort to stay in shape and build a few muscles as well.

In the next few pages you'll find some specific exercises to try, along with a list of Heavenly health clubs, and The Angelic Diet.

Wing Workouts

Until coming to the Afterlife, you may have thought of getting your wings as liberating. Strap on a tiny, gossamer-sheer flapping apparatus and flutter off.

In your dreams.

Wings present all manner of adjustment difficulties. For one thing, parallel parking is a nightmare. But mostly, they put a tremendous strain on one's entire upper body, especially the shoulders, neck, and back.

Hence it is recommended that novice angels work out daily, and include the following in their repertoire:

30 chin-ups
▼
50 neck rolls
▼
100 bicep curls (minimum of 6 lbs. free weights)
▼
100 tricep presses (minimum of 10 lbs. free weights)
▼
150 pelvic tilts
▼
150 abdominal crunches

As Satan likes to say, "Go for the burn!"

The Halo Toss

A halo is a luminous band of light which adorns angels' heads and which contains an energy that continually connects them with Heaven even if they choose to roam elsewhere, say Cleveland. They weigh a fair amount due to the huge number of D batteries necessary to keep then charged with Divine Energy.

For general aerobic fitness we find it is efficient to use the halo itself as an exercise aid—sort of a combination Frisbee and medicine ball:

> With a partner, run laps around the Pearly Gates.
> As you pass each fence post, hurl your halo
> at your fellow angel and run underneath the halo
> aimed at you—so as to catch it with your head.

A three to four time per week regime of halo-tossing is recommended. For variety, try a game of Halo Horsehoes.

Heavenly Health Clubs

Amazing Grace—Specializing in slimnastics and dance aerobics this Goddess-owned and operated fitness center prides itself not only on trimming and toning but on teaching its patrons impeccable angelic posture.

Lourdes—Sprained your sciatica or crunched your clavicle trying to get airborne? Spend an afternoon in a Lourdes Miracle Mud Bath or being shiatsued by an Angel of Mercy.

We Shall Overcome—Hard-core bench-pressers and body builders frequent this no-frills, no-nonsense gym where the head instructor is a former Mr. Universe.

Marching To Pretoria—Low impact routines for those new to exercise or who are prone to shin splints.

Firmament—If you don't look fabulous in a thong leotard you'll probably feel a tad out of place in this super-trendy fitness establishment. But the juice bar is a great place just to hang out, ogle, and down a Heavenly Health Shake.

The Angelic Diet

If you find you need to trim a few pounds off those cherubic thighs in a hurry, we recommend this quick and easy seven day weight loss plan.

Breakfast

Holy Water
Wafers

Lunch

Salad with *Saved-By-the-Light Mayo.*

Snack

One piece unleavened bread.

Dinner

Serene Cuisine frozen entreé.
Wine optional.

IX

Special Situations

So many of you have written to us with specific questions regarding your individual concerns about the Afterlife that we thought we would reproduce some of those letters in the following pages. Hopefully our answers may be of use to others with similar concerns.

Dear Visitor's Guide:

I need to know if we ultimately meet all our loved ones in the Afterlife. Because, you see, I've had a lot of, er, loved ones. You see there was my dear wife Gladys, but then of course there was Bubbles and Flo and Gloria and that temporary secretary, the one who smelled like gardenias, and there was . . . Well, you catch my drift. Not all of them might enjoy getting to know one another. It could be rather awkward, don't you think?

Signed,
Phil Landerer

Dear Phil:

As a matter of fact, all loved ones—yes, all—are eventually reunited in the Afterlife. They will probably enjoy meeting one another very much. And they'll have endless time to compare notes.

The Guide

Dear Visitor's Guide:

I'd always read in the Bible that God was big on "testing" people. Take Abraham, for example, and the whole first-born child thing. What I am wondering is are there any tests in the Afterlife, and should I be studying now?

Signed,
Compulsive Overachiever

Dear Overachiever:

Well, now that you mention it . . . the Almighty does like to spring a pop quiz now and again featuring such brain-teasers as:

If God created the Universe, what existed before the Universe began?

A) A point of matter so dense as to contain all matter that exists everywhere.
B) Blueprints
C) Pure Unconditional Love
D) Universe-In-A-Box
E) the Lord's Lego set

So sorry, we are not allowed to divulge the correct answer.

The Guide

Dear Visitor's Guide:

I always imagined Heaven would be nice and quiet. But the din is eternally annoying. If it's not the elves, it's the reindeer. If it's not the reindeer, it's those blasted sugar-plum fairies. And what's with the "Ho, Ho, Ho?"

Signed,
In Need of Earplugs

Dear Earplugs:

Heaven *would* be peaceful—if you were there.
You were supposed to take a *left* at the harps. Tell Santa what you want for Christmas and try again.

The Guide

Dear Visitor's Guide:

Now that I'm in Heaven, do I still have to go to church on Sunday? It seems a little redundant.

Signed,
Likes To Sleep In

Dear Likes To Sleep:

In a way you're right. There is a kind of coals-to-Newcastle quality about attending church in Heaven. And the Almighty, as you may have heard, also likes to enjoy a good snooze on the Sabbath.

The Guide

Dear Visitor's Guide:

Ouch. I think I just fractured my wing. Where's the closest emergency room?

Signed,
Clumsy

Dear Clumsy:

St. Elsewhere.

The Guide

Dear Visitor's Guide:

Can I be represented by an attorney on my Day of Judgment. And is the verdict subject to appeals?

Signed,
Litigious

Dear Litigious:

There are no *lawyers* in Heaven. You can't get a continuance, can't plea bargain, can't file for a mistrial. Your best bet: Throw yourself on the Mercy of the Court, or find a white Bronco and run for it.

The Guide

Dear Visitor's Guide:

Will I be reunited with my lifetime's worth of cherished pets in the Afterlife? And, if so, how will I ever take care of them all?

Signed,
Animal Lover

Dear Animal Lover:

As of this writing, no pets are allowed in Heaven proper, although they do reside in a nearby animal sanctuary. However, there is a major animals rights movement underway led by trendsetter Saint Francis of Assisi. We'll keep you posted.

The Guide

Dear Visitor's Guide:

Can I use my Frequent Flyer miles to get to the Afterlife.

Signed,
Standby

Dear Standby:

Yes, especially if they are on U.S. Air.

The Guide

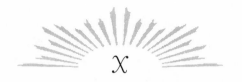

X

If You're Thinking of Coming Back

A Visitor's Query: This Eternity stuff is all very nice. But I do sometimes think about the life I had before and those I left behind. What if I want to pay a brief visit to an earth-bound loved one? And what if I want to go back and rejoin the World?

The Guide Responds: There are indeed some ways to make contact with the folks back on Earth while remaining in the Afterlife oneself, though one must be discreet when "phoning home," as we shall explain.

As for returning to Earth in a physical body, there are two possibilities. First, you may discover during your travels that you are not permanently dead at all, but only the victim of a near-death experience. If this is the case, we will in the following pages suggest a few things you might bring back with you to help you earn your fifteen minutes of Earthly fame.

Second, depending on your personal philosophy, you may find you have the option to dabble at the game of life again in another "incarnation." If so, we will suggest some new personae you may wish to try on for size.

Phoning Home: Some Ways to Check In With Those You Left Behind

If you've become a permanent resident in the Afterlife, telecommunications with loved ones back on Earth are not as accessible as you might have hoped. In Eternity, AT&T (Almighty's Telepathy & and Telekinesis) still has a monopoly. So if you'd like to drop in on a still-living spouse, friend, coworker or what have you, you need to use one of His indirect, ethereal methods. Among your choices are:

Becoming a Ghost—Hey, Patrick Swayze did it, so why can't you? It takes a while—and a few nasty black and blues—before you'll walk through walls with ease. But once you've got the knack, wow. Plus, the invisibility factor is great for eavesdropping. The downside: AT&T haunting rates are very steep, which is why most haunting is done in off-peak hours, between midnight and 4 A.M.

Becoming a Poltergeist—A great way to settle old scores with former bosses, two-timing boyfriends, pesky IRS auditors and the like. Become a bona fide nuisance! Fling prized vases and family heirlooms about. Rearrange furniture when no one is looking. Empty file drawers and crash hard drives. Best of all, if you're especially gifted at this, you may be offered a cameo in a Spielberg movie

Finding a Channeler—Too shy to haunt? Too polite to chuck a priceless Ming vase into the fireplace? Then perhaps

AT&T's channeling service is for you. First it's necessary to find a willing medium (Whoopi Goldberg is obliging, but very pricey). This person will transcribe your messages while they are in a trance state. Of late, many popular books have been channeled as folks from the Afterlife often feel they have a good deal to pontificate about.

Becoming a Muse—If you like to hang around creative types, and if you've always wanted a chance to express yourself, inspire a struggling painter, writer, or musician. Here is your chance to do your bit for the arts.

Doing a Stint as a Guardian Angel—Now that you've met and thanked your own guardian angel, you may wish to take a turn guiding and protecting someone back on Earth. But keep in mind, the hours are very long, the pay low, the responsibility and stress factors very high—especially if you wind up in charge of, say, your idiot brother-in-law who likes to impress his dates by skydiving, bungie jumping, and antagonizing steroid-crazed bouncers at the local micro-brewery.

Ooops, You Weren't *Really* Dead . . .

Son of a gun, the night nurse tripped over the cord that was attached to your respirator and then left to go on her break. For a while there they thought you were a goner, but you were really off having the travel experience of a lifetime. Now you just have to prove it. Herewith, a list of suggested items to bring back from your near-death experience:

1. New outfit for guest appearance on *Oprah.*

2. Ghostwriter.

3. Agent.

4. Cryptic messages and assorted revelations regarding the millennium.

5. T-shirts.

6. "Been there, done that" bumper stickers.

7. "My Original Sin" perfume samples.

8. "Tree of Knowledge" home version board game.

9. A new attitude.

10. A tan.

If You're Thinking of Reincarnating . . .

On the other hand, maybe you did really die, but you'd like to give Earth another go. If so, reincarnation may be for you—providing you can get the Almighty's okay. Once that's accomplished, there are many choices to ponder for your next go-round on the planet. When selecting who or what you'd like to return as, you may wish to consider the following identities—each with its own advantages and disadvantages:

Astronaut—Gets you the closest you can be to the heavens without entering the Afterlife. On the other hand, the food is lousy and you have to answer nature's call in your suit.

Billionaire—Obvious advantages include loads of bucks, assorted mansions and yachts. But the taxes may kill you.

Football Hero—The glory, the glamour, the high-paying endorsements. The shattered kneecaps, the steroids, those god-awful Superbowl half-times. Plus you have to listen to Frank Gifford go on about Cody . . .

First Lady—You'll have to contend with rumors that your husband cheats on you, or that you're a megalomaniac pulling the strings behind the scenes. They'll say your hairdo is dowdy and that you're no Jackie. At the same time, those Secret Service guys are pretty hunky . . .

First Family's Pet—Perhaps you'd like to do a stint in the animal kingdom. What better choice than to come back as the beloved kitty or canine who lives in the White House? You can fetch a stick in the Rose Garden, or cough up a fur ball in the Oval office. On the other hand, you can't get a date.

Algae—For those of you who crave the simple life. The *real* simple life. The downside: no one likes to be called pond scum.

XI

The Afterlife Satisfaction Survey

About the Survey

You'd think everyone would be happy about the Afterlife's existence, given the exceptionally dreary alternative. (Ashes to ashes . . . *what* a downer.) And most folks are pretty darned pleased to see the proverbial light at the end of the Tunnel.

But, of course, even Paradise isn't perfect—and some souls are more picky than others. Hence, we bring you the official Visitor's Guide Afterlife Satisfaction Survey, which we believe offers a fair overview of how people *really* feel about Life After Death, and what suggestions they have for making it even better than it is today. . . .

The Afterlife Satisfaction Survey

How would you rate Heaven in terms of overall ambience?
 Awe-inspiring—43%
 Glorious—36%
 A Little Dull—21%

Which of these changes do you believe might result in the greatest improvement?
 More ethnic restaurants—19%
 More racquetball facilities—12%
 More moderately priced hotels—18%
 Less red tape—51%

How do you feel you were dealt with on your Day of Judgment?
 Overall, pretty fair and square—75%
 A bum rap—5%
 I miss my lawyer!—20%

What was the biggest problem you had in adjusting to angelhood?
 Can no longer sleep on your back—43%
 Hard to keep your hat on—27%
 Too much publicity—30%

What do you miss most about life on Earth?
    Monday night football—46%
    Home Shopping Network—38%
    Sex—16%

Are there any improvements you think should be made in the Hell side trip?
    More snow cone stands—23%
    Quicker air-conditioning repair service—43%
    Something else on the Muzak system besides "Sympathy for the Devil"—34%

Are there any improvements you think should be made in the Limbo side trip?
    Shouldn't last Forever and a Day—52%
    Hate that *Charlie's Angels* ripoff, *Limbo's Bimbos*—21%
    Something else on Muzak besides calypso—27%

Overall how would you rate the Almighty as a host?
    Very gracious—77%
    Somewhat gracious—13%
    He's no Martha Stewart—10%

If you could send the folks back on Earth one message about coming to the Afterlife, what would it be?
    Hurry up—56%
    Take your time—18%
    Bring up a *People* magazine and some beer nuts—26%

XII

An Interview with the Almighty

Since Afterlife dwellers have had their say, it seemed only fair to elicit some comments from the Almighty himself. Hence, the *Visitor's Guide* dispensed a reporter to chat with Him. Getting in to see Him was no simple matter, as His calendar is so jammed. Also, His publicity agent, the Archangel Michael, was insistent that questions be submitted for review ahead of time. However, we trust you will nevertheless find the following enlightening.

An Interview with the Almighty

VG: *Why did you create both Life on Earth and the Afterlife?*

  G: Variety.

VG: *But why must we endure the sufferings of earthly existence before entering Paradise? Why can't we all be in Paradise always.*

  G: Maximum Occupancy Regulations. What did you think, Eternity goes on forever?

VG: *You mean there's something beyond Infinity?*

  G: That's for me to know and you to find out.

VG: *Okay...so, about you and Lucifer. What really happened?*

  G: No comment.

VG: *You seem to be a Deity of few words. Do you like speaking in paradoxes, or are you perhaps a bit shy?*

  G: Actually, I'm just pretending I'm Warren Beatty.

VG: *Oh. Back to more cosmic concerns. Can you tell us anything about what happened before the Big Bang.*

  G: How should I know? I was taking a nap.

VG: *So you don't remember anything about what existed beforehand?*

  G: Well, there was some warm milk, percale sheets, and a nice down comforter.

VG: *And when the Big Bang occurred—what do you recall about that?*

  G: What a racket. Ka-blam. Ka-bloom. It could have woken Snow White.

VG: *And after the Universe was created, You created Man, right?*

G: Yes, and woman. Don't forget. They get very upset if you forget.

VG: *So, what do you think of your handiwork?*

G: Still a few glitches. Like the whole childbirth thing. I've had some complaints, you know.

VG: *Why did you evict Adam and Eve from the Garden of Eden?*

G: It was time to renovate. Plus, I think they were planning to sublet illegally.

VG: *Did you give them any guidelines for behavior on Earth other than "the Ten Commandments?"*

G: Actually, there were eleven. Something got lost in the translation.

VG: *What was the Eleventh?*

G: No personal checks on the express line at the supermarket.

VG: *That's it?*

G: Yes, it's *so* inconsiderate.

VG: *I'll be sure to pass that along. And do you have any other advice for us?*

G: Sure. Dying is easy, but comedy is hard.

VG: *Anything else?*

G: A bird in the hand is worth two in the bush. Don't put all your eggs in one basket. I got a million of 'em.

VG: *I bet you do but we're out of time. . . .*

G: Don't count your chickens before they're hatched. Keep your chin up and your nose to the grindstone. A stitch in time saves nine—

VG: *Thank you, Lord.*

G: Say, did you hear the one about . . .

Amen.